Merry Christmas Journal

A Fun Fill-in Book for Kids

Diana Zourelias

Dover Publications, Inc.
Mineola, New York

This journal belongs to:

_____

Date: *Reega*

Bibliographical Note

My Merry Christmas Journal: A Fun Fill-in Book for Kids is a new work,
first published by Dover Publications, Inc., in 2019.

International Standard Book Number

ISBN-13: 978-0-486-83307-1
ISBN-10: 0-486-83307-0

Manufactured in the United States by LSC Communications
83307001   2019
www.doverpublications.com

Santa's Reindeer are named Dasher, Dancer, Prancer, Vixen, Comet, Cupid, Donner, Blitzen and Rudolph. If Santa added another Reindeer, I think it should be named _COCO_.

_____ .

This is a drawing of
what I want my
Gingerbread House
to look like!

Santa Always wears the Same Clothes! This is what he would Look like if I Could Dress Him!

Rather than put
an ELF on a
Shelf...

I would put Mine:

_____
_____
_____

Because ————————————————
_____
_____
_____
_____.

4

I wonder what Mrs. Claus's
First Name is? I think that

---

would be PERFECT!

Just about Everyone leaves Santa cookies for his Christmas Visit. I want to be a little more Creative! I'm going to leave Santa:

Nachos and Cheese
Pizza
Gummy Worms
Chips and Dip
Burger and Fries
Box of Chocolates
Fruit Salad
Other —————————————

Candy Canes are usually Striped.

If I could redesign a Candy Cane it would look like...

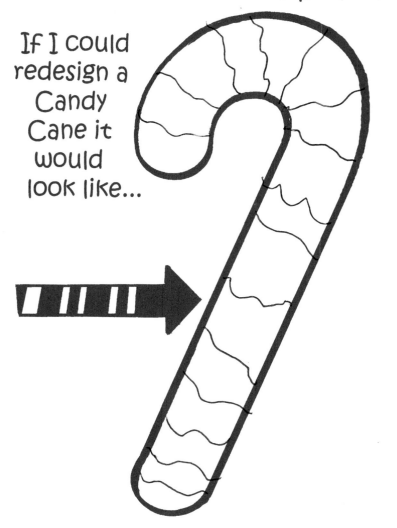

It's Fun to Decorate
Christmas Cookies!
Aren't mine Beautiful?
(Add some cookie shapes
of your own!)

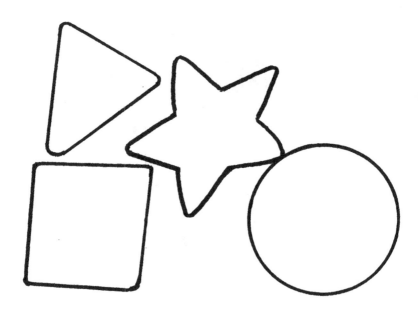

Not Everyone has a Chimney!

If Santa can't get down our Chimney,
maybe he can try Leaving Gifts...

☐ With the Mail Carrier

☐ On the Window sills

☐ At the Front Door

☐ Outside our Apartment

☐ In the Garage

☐ In our Family Car

☐ In the Backyard

☐ Other _____

9

This is a drawing of my Christmas Card...

...and a list of People I will send it to...

Name: Reese Smith
Address: _____

_____

Name: Harper Smith
Address: _____

_____

Name: micLsmith
Address: _____

_____

Name: cristymith
Address: _____

_____

Name: Danyollsmith
Address: _____

_____

Name: _____
Address: _____

_____

Santa's Hair and Beard
look PERFECT... but I
decided to see what he'd
look like with a Makeover!

Santa's Ride needs an Update! Here's a Picture of what he should be Driving!

Whew! Santa had a Long
Night! This is what I think
he does on December 26th.

_____

_____

_____

_____

_____

_____

_____

FOR:
SANTA

Every year Santa
brings US Gifts!
This year I am
going to leave
him This Gift:

_____

Because

15

I've Created my own Ornament!

I get so Excited on Christmas Eve
that I Can Never Fall Asleep!
This year I am going to Play a Game.
How Many Words Can you make out
of the Word

ChrISTMAS

_____   _____

_____   _____

_____   _____

_____   _____

_____   _____

_____   _____

_____   _____

_____   _____

_____   _____

This is what I did Every Day Leading to the Best Day of the Year!

DECEMBER

1	2	3	4	5
6	7	8	9	10
11	12	13	14	15
16	17	18	19	20
21	22	23	24	25

Every Snowflake is Different, and this is Mine!

My Christmas Stocking Looks like This:

And this is What I hope will be in it!!!

_____

_____

_____

_____

_____

_____

_____

_____

_____

_____

_____

_____

This is a List Of Questions I have for Santa in case I ever Interview him!

_____
_____
_____
_____
_____
_____
_____
_____
_____
_____

Santa has a Naughty and Nice List...this is the One Naughty Thing I hope he (and my Parents) Don't find out about!

_____

_____

_____

_____

_____

_____

_____

_____

_____

_____

I watch All the Christmas
Cartoon Shows!
My Favorite is _FROSTY_
The SNOWMAN
Because _____
_____
_____
_____ .

24

Hot Chocolate is a Yummy Holiday Treat! I like to add...

Candy Canes

Marshmallows

Sprinkles

Whipped Cream

Chocolate Chips

Peppermint Sticks

All!!!

Other

_____

_____

_____

Match the Christmas Joke with the Punchline on p. 27!

1. What do you call a Cat on the Beach on Christmas Morning?

2. Where do Snowmen keep their Money?

3. What did one Snowman say to the Other?

4. Knock Knock!
Who's there?
Dexter.
Dexter who?

5. What do Elves do After School?

A. Dexter Halls with
   Boughs of Holly.
   ⊦ ∧|∧|ρ|⊦

B. Their Gnome Work.

C. Do you Smell Carrots?

D. Sandy Claws!

E. In a Snow Bank.

Sparkles and Glitter!!!
Christmas should Glow!!!
If I could add Glitter to
things that Don't have
any, I would add it to:

_____   _____

_____   _____

_____   _____

_____   _____

_____   _____

Let it Snow! Let it Snow! Let it Snow!
If it Snows during my Vacation,
I will Definitely:

Build a Snowman

Go Sledding

Make Snow Angels

Have Snowball Fights

Build an Igloo

Other __CA THING__
SNOW=IAke
ON Yo R
TO UNGe

The thing that Annoys me Most about the Holidays is:

- Cleaning my Room.
- Cleaning Anything!
- Going to Bed Early on Christmas Eve.
- Leaving the House (and Gifts!) on Christmas Day.
- Dressing up.
- Not touching the "Good Snacks" that are for Company.
- Other _____

Many People
Decorate
their Homes
with
Scented Candles.
I would like my Candles
to Smell Like:

1. Chocolate
2. Bubble Gum
3. Puppy Breath
4. Popcorn
5. Hamburgers
6. Peppermint
7. Pumpkin Pie
8. Cookies

9. Pizza
10. Sneakers
11. Licorice
12. Pine Tree
13. Kitty Litter
14. Snow
15. Money
Other_____

Every Year I get New Christmas Pajamas (Some years are Better than Others!). If I could Design my own, they would look like this.

If I could Borrow
one of Santa's
Elves for a
week, I'd
have him
Help me with:
- Chores
- Homework
- Gift Buying
- Walking the Dog
- Eating my Brussels Sprouts
- Gift Wrapping
- Making Snacks
- Telling Knock Knock
  Jokes
- Other_____

I wish I had Santa's Cell Phone Number so I could:

 Send him my Wish List

 Send him a Selfie

 Text him my Address for his GPS

 Update him on my Nice List

 Other _____

There seems to be a MISTAKE!!! One thing I have wished for Every Christmas and have yet to Receive is a:

Unicorn
My Own Room
4 Wheeler
Spaceship
Gaming System
Other_____

Dog
Castle
95" TV
Zoo
Horse

_____

35

The Gift I'd like the MOST this Christmas is _____

_____

_____

_____. I think I deserve it Because _____

_____

_____.

FOR: ME

The Best
Gift I ever
got for
Christmas
was

_____

_____

_____

_____

The Worst
Gift was

_____

_____

_____

_____

My Fave Food to eat on Christmas is

_____

and here's how You Make it!

Recipe for 🎄 _____
_____
_____

Ingredients: _____
_____ _____
_____ _____
_____ _____
_____

Directions: _____
_____
_____
_____
_____
_____

If I drew a Picture of it for a Cookbook,
It would look like . . .

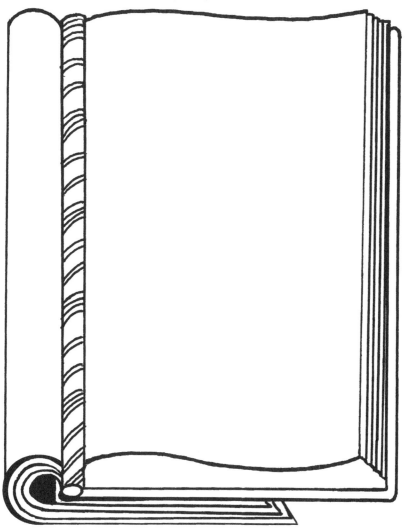

3 Things I could
DO to make

_____

Happy on Christmas
are:

1.————————————

————————————

2.————————————

————————————

3.————————————

It would make me
feel————————————

Here is a Happy Picture of _____.

(Draw or paste Picture here.)

My Favorite Christmas
Tradition is _____
_____
Because_____
_____
_____.
My Least Favorite
Tradition is_____
_____
Because_____
_____.

Here's a List of my Favorite Holiday Songs!

Here's a List of Holiday Songs I Never want to Hear Again!

If I were to go
Christmas Caroling
I would want to stand:

Up Front ———
Way in the Back ———
Right in the Middle ———
Behind a tall person ———

My All-time Favorite Christmas
Movie is _____

_____

I think I have watched it
_____ times! My Favorite
Part is_____.I'd
LOVE to play the Part of____

_____.

Here's a Photo (or Drawing) of our Decorated Family Christmas Tree!

This is a Drawing of what MY Decorated Christmas Tree will look like!

If I could Travel Anywhere in the World for Christmas, I'd go to _____

_____

Because _____

_____.

The One Special Thing we do as a Family over the Holidays is:

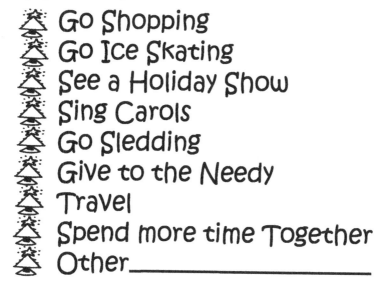

Go Shopping
Go Ice Skating
See a Holiday Show
Sing Carols
Go Sledding
Give to the Needy
Travel
Spend more time Together
Other_____

Here are some Gift Ideas
for Special People
in my Life:

Name: _____

Gift Idea: _____

Name: _____

Gift Idea: _____

Name: _____

Gift Idea: _____

Name: _____

Gift Idea: _____

Name: _____

Gift Idea: _____

Name: _____
Gift Idea: _____

Name: _____
Gift Idea: _____

Name: _____
Gift Idea: _____

Name: _____
Gift Idea: _____

Name: _____
Gift Idea: _____

Name: _____
Gift Idea: _____

Homemade Gifts are Great! Here's a list of Gifts I made and Who they are for:

Name:_____
Gift:_____
_____

Name:_____
Gift:_____
_____

Name:_____
Gift:_____
_____

Name:_____
Gift:_____
_____

Name:_____
Gift:_____
_____

Name:_____
Gift:_____
_____

The Weather on Christmas Day is Usually:
(pick which ones apply)

Hot _____

Cold _____

Sunny _____

Rainy _____

Snowy _____

Windy _____

Foggy _____

Or _____ where I live.

I Like it _____

I Don't like it _____

Because _____

_____.

One of the Best Christmas Stories I ever Read (or Heard!) is _____

_____
_____.

It's about _____

_____
_____
_____
_____
_____.

I LOVE certain Christmas TV Specials that air Every Year! One of my Favorites is_____

_____

Because _____

_____.

My Least Favorite is_____

_____

_____

When I wake up on
Christmas Morning I
Feel_____.
When I wake up the
day After Christmas I
Feel_____.

The First Person I will
Call or text to tell what
I got for Christmas is

_____ .

The First Person I will Call
or Text to wish a Merry
Christmas is _____

_____ .

If I were in a Christmas Play,
I'd be Great at playing the
Part of_____

_____

Because_____

_____

_____

_____

_____ .

My Favorite Christmas Sounds are:

- Carolers
- Music Playing
- Presents being wrapped
  (or unwrapped!)
- Laughter
- Bells Ringing
- Logs Crackling in Fireplace
- Boots Crunching in Snow
  Other _____

Ahhh! If I close my eyes I can Remember some of my Favorite Christmas Smells:

Peppermint
Pine Tree
Fresh Cookies
Cloves
Turkey
Fresh Pies
Fresh Bread
Hot Cocoa

Other_____
_____

This is my Idea of a Perfect Christmas Eve!

_____
_____
_____
_____
_____
_____
_____
_____
_____
_____
_____

This is my Idea of a
Perfect
Christmas!

_____
_____
_____
_____
_____
_____
_____
_____
_____
_____
_____ .

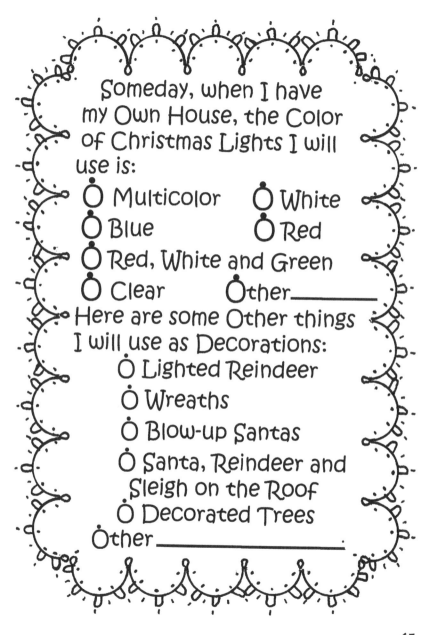

Someday, when I have my Own House, the Color of Christmas Lights I will use is:

○ Multicolor   ○ White
○ Blue   ○ Red
○ Red, White and Green
○ Clear   ○ Other_____

Here are some Other things I will use as Decorations:

○ Lighted Reindeer
○ Wreaths
○ Blow-up Santas
○ Santa, Reindeer and Sleigh on the Roof
○ Decorated Trees
○ Other_____.

63

Not Everyone's as Lucky as Me so
I try to Give Back at Christmas
time and be Generous to Others.
Here's a few Examples: _____

_____

_____

_____

_____

_____

_____

_____

_____ .

I started Planning
for Christmas
and Buying
Gifts
this year
around
(Date)

_____

_____

Next Year I will
Do the Same ____
Start Earlier ____
Start Later ____
Skip it! ____

65

If I threw a Christmas Party I would Invite:

This is the Food I would Serve:

_____   _____
_____   _____
_____   _____
_____   _____
_____

These are some Games we could Play: _____

_____   _____
_____   _____
_____   _____
_____   _____

Here is a Selfie of Me
waiting for Santa!

I know that **Santa** has his **Reindeer** but I think he should have Another **Pet(s)**:

- Polar Bear
- Puppy
- Kitty
- Hamster
- Penguin
- Iguana
- Puffin
- Other_____

Because _____ .

I LOVE playing Secret Santa!
I play it with:

 Classmates

Family

Friends

Cousins

Other

This is Who I got this Year: _____
_____ and what I Bought: ___

_____

This is a list of People I will be Video Chatting with on Christmas Day: _____

_____   _____

_____   _____

_____   _____

_____   _____

I think my Family should have
an UGLY SWEATER PARTY!
Here's what mine would
Look like!

SHHHH!!!! Please Keep a Secret! This is a List of things I Like at Christmas that would Surprise most People:

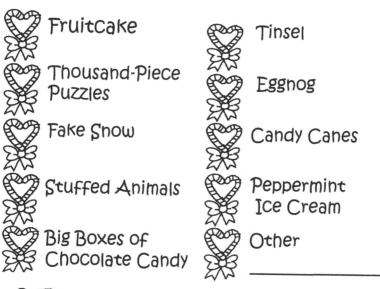

- Fruitcake
- Thousand-Piece Puzzles
- Fake Snow
- Stuffed Animals
- Big Boxes of Chocolate Candy
- Tinsel
- Eggnog
- Candy Canes
- Peppermint Ice Cream
- Other _____

YUM.

FRUITCAKE

These are some of the Activities
I am looking forward to during
Christmas Vacation:

- ☆ Sleeping
- ☆ Returning some Gifts
- ☆ Eating Leftovers
- ☆ Going to the Movies
- ☆ Sleepovers
- ☆ Playing Video Games
- ☆ Reading a Good Book
- ☆ Hanging out with Friends
- ☆ Going to the Movies
- ☆ Other _____

ZZZ..

The ONE Thing I can count on Getting as a Christmas Gift is

_____

It's Usually From:

I LOVE Snow Globes! (especially the ones with Music!) Here's my Design for one...

and the Song it Plays is _____

_____

Santa Cash

Santa Claus

If I get some
MONEY as a
Christmas Gift
I Plan to:
1. Save it for
Something BIG
2. Buy _____
_____
_____
ASAP!

Paste a Christmas Selfie in this Frame.

Then add a Funny Caption!

I LOVE making Christmas Decorations!

These are a Few of the Ones I made This Year:

- Paper Chains
- Paper Snowflakes
- Popcorn Snowmen
- Clothespin People or Snowmen
- Paperplate Art
- Other

My Parents think that a
Good Place to Hide
Christmas Presents is

_____

but MY Hiding Place is
Much Better! No one
will ever look _____

_____ .

On Christmas Morning
I'd Love to open the
Front Door and see

Standing there!

The Gifts in the Holiday Song "The 12 Days of Christmas" are very Old-Fashioned. So I changed them:

1 Partridge in a Pear Tree

1._____

2 Turtle Doves

2._____
_____

3 French Hens

3._____
_____

4 Calling Birds

4._____
_____

5 Golden Rings

5._____
_____

6 Geese-a-Laying

6._____
_____

7 Swans-a-Swimming

7. _____

_____

8 Maids-a-Milking

8. _____

_____

9 Ladies
Dancing

9. _____

_____

10 Lords-a-Leaping

10. _____

_____

11 Pipers
Piping

11. _____

_____

12 Drummers Drumming

12. _____

_____

The one Thing I can do WITHOUT on Christmas Morning is:

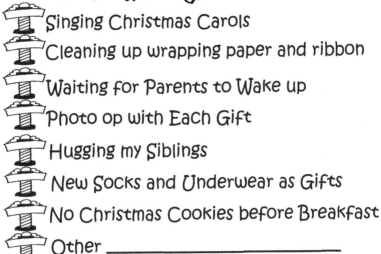

- Singing Christmas Carols
- Cleaning up wrapping paper and ribbon
- Waiting for Parents to Wake up
- Photo op with Each Gift
- Hugging my Siblings
- New Socks and Underwear as Gifts
- No Christmas Cookies before Breakfast
- Other _____

This is the One Thing I did on Christmas that made me PROUD...

_____
_____
_____
_____
_____
_____
_____
_____

My Parents are GREAT at keeping the house Well Stocked with Holiday Supplies Except for:

FZZZZZZZTTT

- Batteries
- Christmas Cookies
- More Gifts for ME
- Chocolate Milk
- Wrapping Paper
- More Christmas Cookies
- Christmas Lights Replacement
- Other_____

Even though I will try NOT to...
One thing that will probably make me Cry during the Holidays is a:

Song _____

Movie _____

Person _____

Commercial _____

Gift _____

Food _____

Memory _____

Other _____

There is Always One House on the Block that Goes Overboard with Christmas Decorations. Here's what it looked like this year!

The Hardest thing NOT to Do on Christmas Day is:

 Burp

 Yawn (after Dinner)

 Hum a Christmas Song

 Play with Gifts

 Be Hugged by a Relative

 Eat Candy

 Other _____

Even though my Pet(s) don't
Know it's Christmas, I always buy

a Special Gift or two. This year
I surprisedHim/Her/Them with:

_____

_____

_____

_____

The ONE GIFT I really wanted
was _____

I got it but ended up being
very Disappointed because

_____

_____

_____

_____

My Letter to Santa! I checked off the Important Stuff.

DEAR SANTA,

Long time NO SEE! I thought I'D DROP YOU A line.
- [ ] DO YOU REMEMBER ME?
- [ ] HOW are YOU & MRS. CLAUS?
- [ ] HAVE YOU BEEN NAUGHTY or NICE?
- [ ] Did You MOVE and Not TELL ME?
- [ ] _____

ONE thing I ALWAYS WONDERED WAS...
- [ ] How TALL ARE You?
- [ ] WHO PAYS YOU?
- [ ] WHO delivers Your Gifts?
- [ ] DO YOU USE A MAP OR A GPS?
- [ ] _____

I wanted to write EARLY...
- [ ] So YOU can Start MAKING MY GIFTS.
- [ ] JUST in CASE You're Lonely.
- [ ] So I can be YOUR First STOP
- [ ] 'CAUSE I'VE been GOOD!
- [ ] _____

92

Let ME KNOW WHAT SNACK You'd like ME to leave You under THE TREE ...

☐ Cookies & MiLK
☐ BURGER 'n FRIES
☐ A TV DINNER
☐ REINDEER FOOD
☐ _____

I DON'T want You to Think ALL I think about is Me, Me, Me...
☐ but it's TRUE!
☐ I think about MY DOG, TOO!
☐ I THINK of YOU, YOU, YOU, Too!
☐ but at least I THINK!
☐ _____

I think you SHOULD GET A 10th REINDEER AND NAME it...

☐ After ME!   ☐ JiNGLeS!
☐ ANY NiCe NAME!
☐ FiDO.
☐ _____

△ MY ADDRESS: (IN CASE YOU FORGET!)

_____
_____
_____

JUST 1 more ☐little☐ FAVOR
I'd like TO ASK OF YOU...
☐ **Please** TAKE A Selfie
with *my* PHONE!
☐ LEAVE **RECEIPTS** So I can
take st**uff** BACK.
☐ TRY ☐NOT☐ to MAKE a MESS.

☐ ————————————————
MY CHRISTMAS LIST:

———————————   ———————————
———————————   ———————————
———————————   ———————————
———————————   ———————————
———————————   ———————————
———————————   ———————————
———————————   ———————————

Your
FRIEND ————————————